KUMON®

MATH. READING. SUCCESS.

What is Kumon?

Kumon is the world's largest supplemental education provider and a leader in producing outstanding results. After-school programs in math and reading at Kumon Centers around the globe have been helping children succeed for 50 years.

Kumon Workbooks represent just a fraction of our complete curriculum of preschool-to-college-level material assigned at Kumon Centers under the supervision of trained Kumon Instructors.

The Kumon Method enables each child to progress successfully by practicing material until concepts are mastered and advancing in small, manageable increments. Instructors carefully assign materials and pace advancement according to the strengths and needs of each individual student.

Students usually attend a Kumon Center twice a week and practice at home the other five days. Assignments take about twenty minutes.

Kumon helps students of all ages and abilities master the basics, improve concentration and study habits, and build confidence.

How did Kumon begin?

IT ALL BEGAN IN JAPAN 50 YEARS AGO when a parent and teacher named Toru Kumon found a way to help his son Takeshi do better in school. At the prompting of his wife, he created a series of short assignments that his son could complete successfully in less than 20 minutes a day and that would ultimately make high school math easy. Because each was just a bit more challenging than the last, Takeshi was able to master the skills and gain the confidence to keep advancing.

This unique self-learning method was so successful that Toru's son was able to do calculus by the time he was in the sixth grade. Understanding the value of good reading comprehension, Mr. Kumon then developed a reading program employing the same method. His programs are the basis and inspiration of those offered at Kumon Centers today under the expert guidance of professional Kumon Instructors.

Mr. Toru Kumon
Founder of Kumon

What can Kumon do for my child?

Kumon is geared to children of all ages and skill levels. Whether you want to give your child a leg up in his or her schooling, build a strong foundation for future studies or address a possible learning problem, Kumon provides an effective program for developing key learning skills given the strengths and needs of each individual child.

What makes Kumon so different?

Kumon uses neither a classroom model nor a tutoring approach. It's designed to facilitate self-acquisition of the skills and study habits needed to improve academic performance. This empowers children to succeed on their own, giving them a sense of accomplishment that fosters further achievement. Whether for remedial work or enrichment, a child advances according to individual ability and initiative to reach his or her full potential. Kumon is not only effective, but also surprisingly affordable.

What is the role of the Kumon Instructor?

Kumon Instructors regard themselves more as mentors or coaches than teachers in the traditional sense. Their principal role is to provide the direction, support and encouragement that will guide the student to performing at 100% of his or her potential. Along with their rigorous training in the Kumon Method, all Kumon Instructors share a passion for education and an earnest desire to help children succeed.

KUMON FOSTERS:

- A mastery of the basics of reading and math
- Improved concentration and study habits
- Increased self-discipline and self-confidence
- A proficiency in material at every level
- Performance to each student's full potential
- A sense of accomplishment

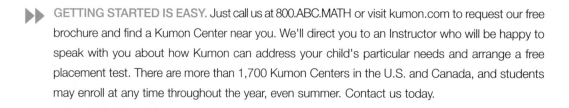

▶▶ GETTING STARTED IS EASY. Just call us at 800.ABC.MATH or visit kumon.com to request our free brochure and find a Kumon Center near you. We'll direct you to an Instructor who will be happy to speak with you about how Kumon can address your child's particular needs and arrange a free placement test. There are more than 1,700 Kumon Centers in the U.S. and Canada, and students may enroll at any time throughout the year, even summer. Contact us today.

Which Is Heavier?

Name

Date

To Parents: If your child does not know which object to color, please tell him or her to color the object that weighs more.

■ Which object is heavier? Color the heavier object.

①

②

③

④

1

■Which object is heavier? Color the heavier object.

①

②

③

④

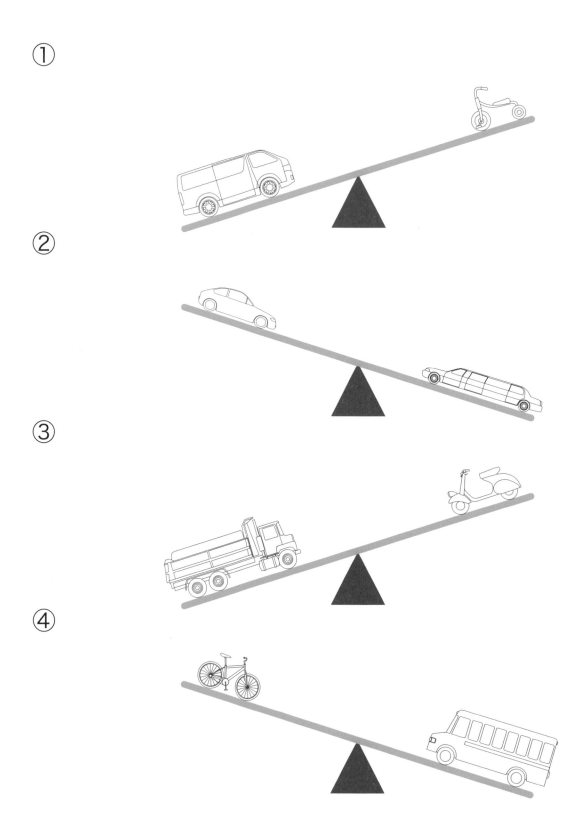

2 Which Is Lighter?

Name

Date

■ Which object is lighter? Color the lighter object.

①

②

③

④

■Which object is lighter? Color the lighter object.

①

②

③

④

Which Is Heaviest?

Name

Date

To Parents: If your child does not know which object to circle, please tell him or her to circle the object that weighs the most.

■ Which object is heaviest? Circle the heaviest object.

①

②

③

④

■Which object is heaviest? Circle the heaviest object.

①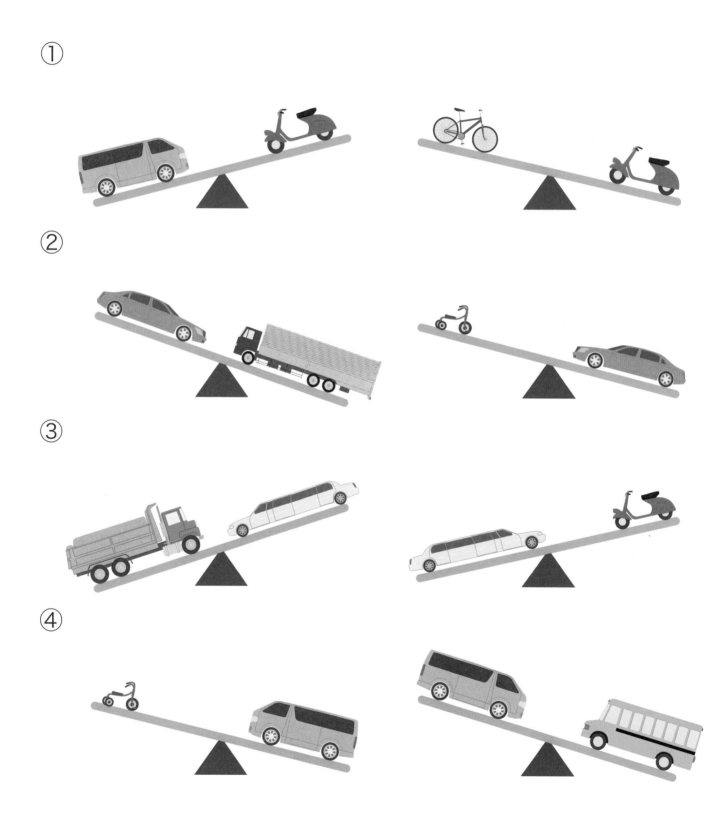

②

③

④

4 Which Is Heaviest?

<table>
<tr><td>Name</td></tr>
<tr><td>Date</td></tr>
</table>

■ Which object is heaviest? Circle the heaviest object.

① ② ③ ④

■Which object is heaviest? Circle the heaviest object.

①

②

③

④

Which Is Lightest?

Name

Date

■ Which object is lightest? Circle the lightest object.

①

②

③

④

■Which object is lightest? Circle the lightest object.

①

②

③

④

6 Which Is Lightest?

■ Which object is lightest? Circle the lightest object.

① ② ③ ④

■Which object is lightest? Circle the lightest object.

①

②

③

④

Which Is Heavier?

Name
Date

■ Each block below is the same size and weight. Color the heavier group of blocks.

①

②

③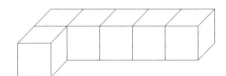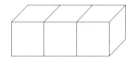

④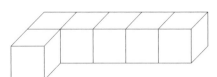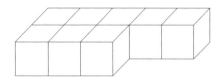

⑤

13

■Each block below is the same size and weight. Color the heavier group of blocks.

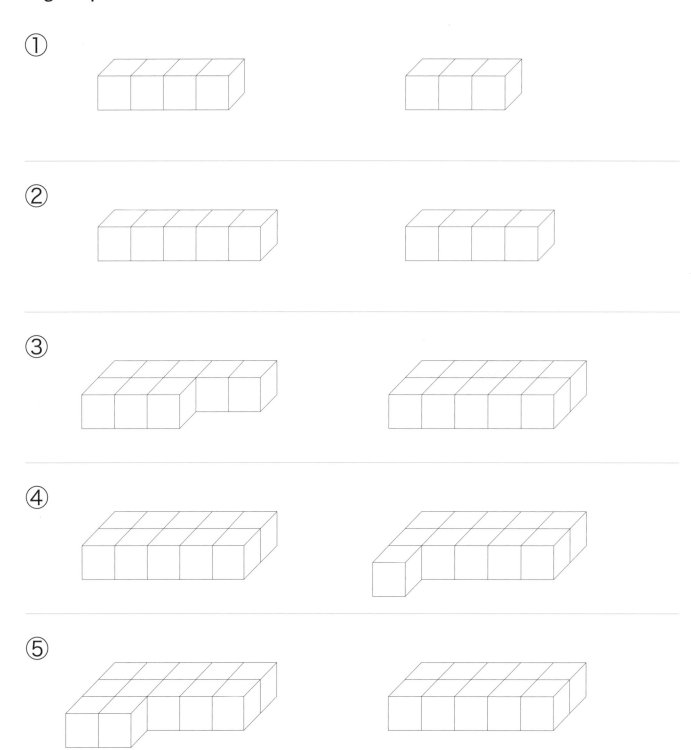

① ② ③ ④ ⑤

14

Which Is Heavier?

Name
Date

■ Each block below is the same size and weight. Color the heavier group of blocks.

①

②

③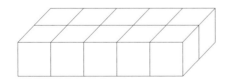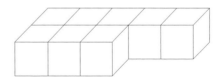

④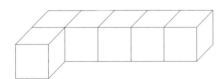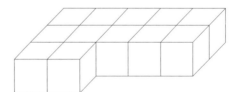

⑤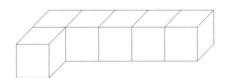

■Each block below is the same size and weight. Color the heavier group of blocks.

①

②

③

④

⑤

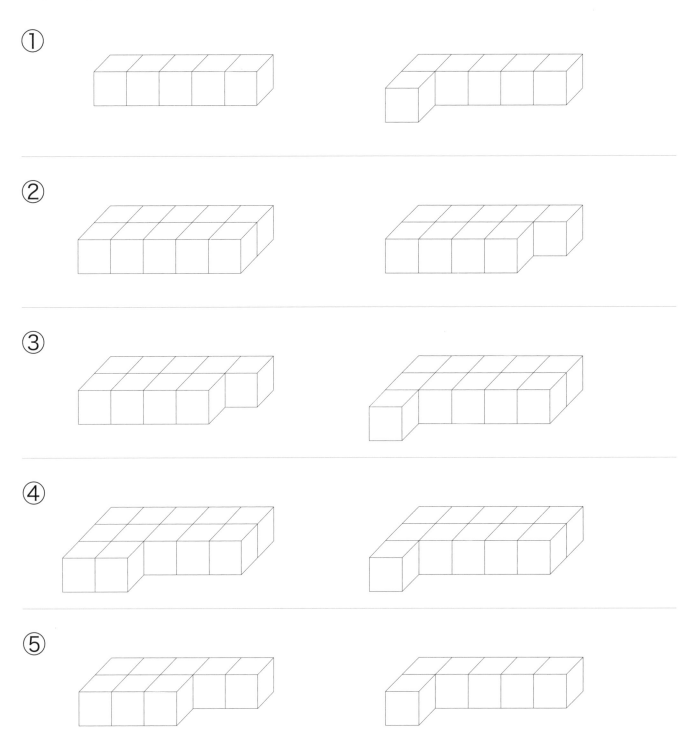

9 Which Is Heavier?

Name
Date

■ Each block below is the same size and weight. Color the heavier group of blocks.

 ①

②

③

④

⑤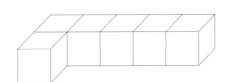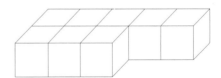

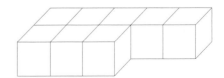

■Each block below is the same size and weight. Color the heavier group of blocks.

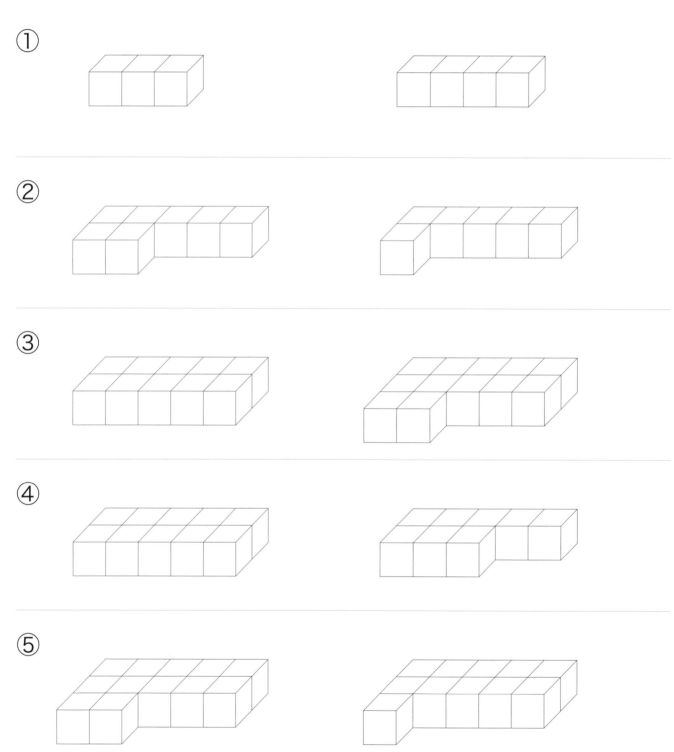

①

②

③

④

⑤

Name

Date

■ Each block below is the same size and weight. Which is the heaviest group, and which is the lightest group below? Write a check (✔) under the heaviest and a circle (○) under the lightest.

①

(○)   (   )   (✔)

②

(   )   (   )   (   )

③

(   )   (   )   (   )

④

(   )   (   )   (   )

⑤

(   )   (   )   (   )

■Each block below is the same size and weight. Which is the heaviest group, and which is the lightest group below? Write a check (✔) under the heaviest and a circle (○) under the lightest.

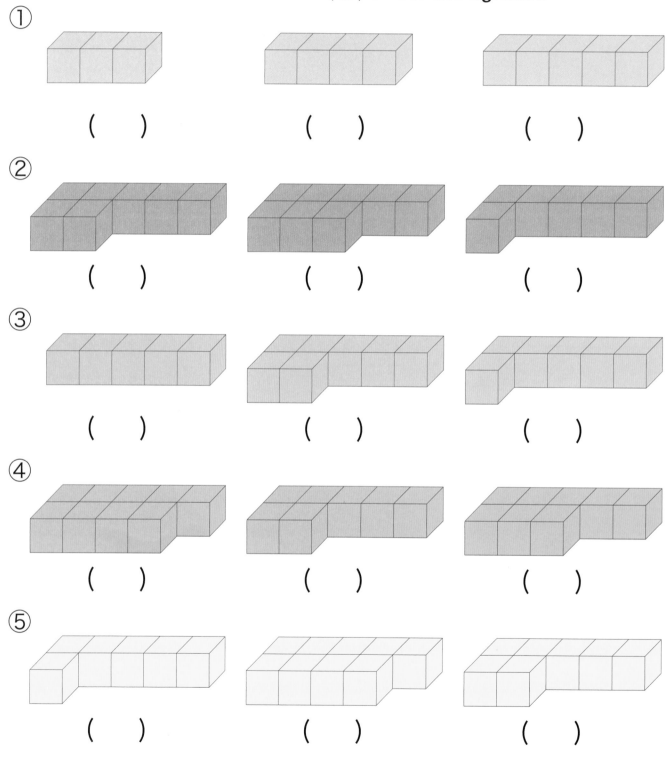

① ( )   ( )   ( )

② ( )   ( )   ( )

③ ( )   ( )   ( )

④ ( )   ( )   ( )

⑤ ( )   ( )   ( )

Name

Date

■ Each block below is the same size and weight. Which is the heaviest group, and which is the lightest group below? Write a check (✔) under the heaviest and a circle (○) under the lightest.

①

(   )   (   )   (   )

②

(   )   (   )   (   )

③

(   )   (   )   (   )

④

(   )   (   )   (   )

⑤

(   )   (   )   (   )

21

■Each block below is the same size and weight. Which is the heaviest group, and which is the lightest group below? Write a check (✔) under the heaviest and a circle (○) under the lightest.

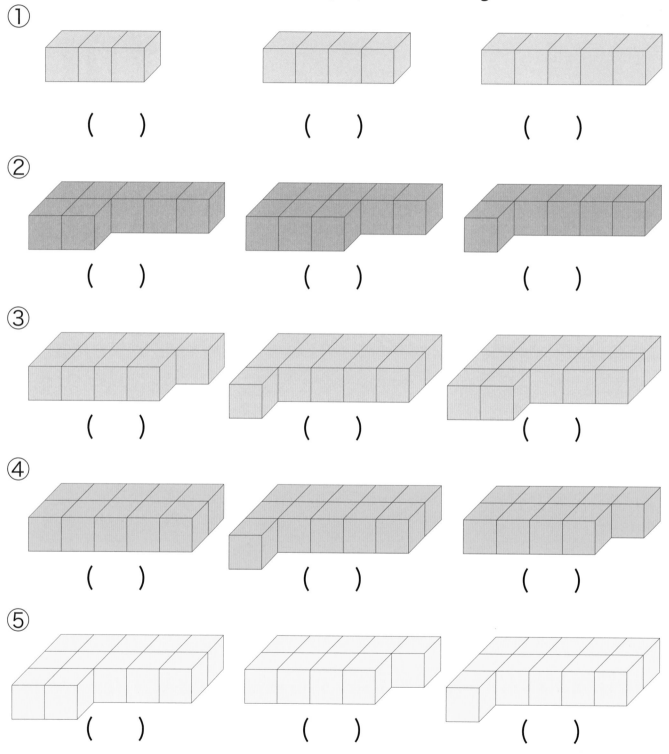

① ( )　　( )　　( )

② ( )　　( )　　( )

③ ( )　　( )　　( )

④ ( )　　( )　　( )

⑤ ( )　　( )　　( )

12 Equal Weights

Name

Date

■ Each block below is the same size and weight. Color the correct number of blocks on the right side to match the weight of the blocks on the left side.

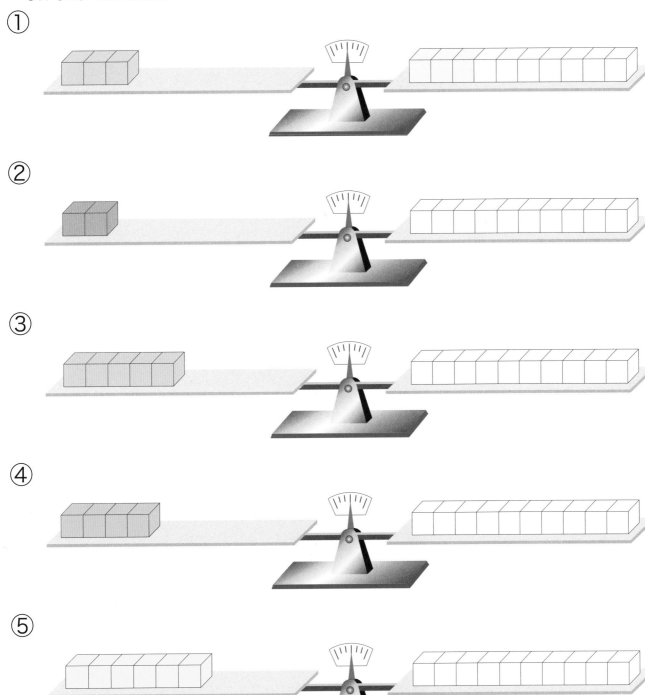

① ② ③ ④ ⑤

■Each block below is the same size and weight. Color the correct number of blocks on the right side to match the weight of the blocks on the left side.

①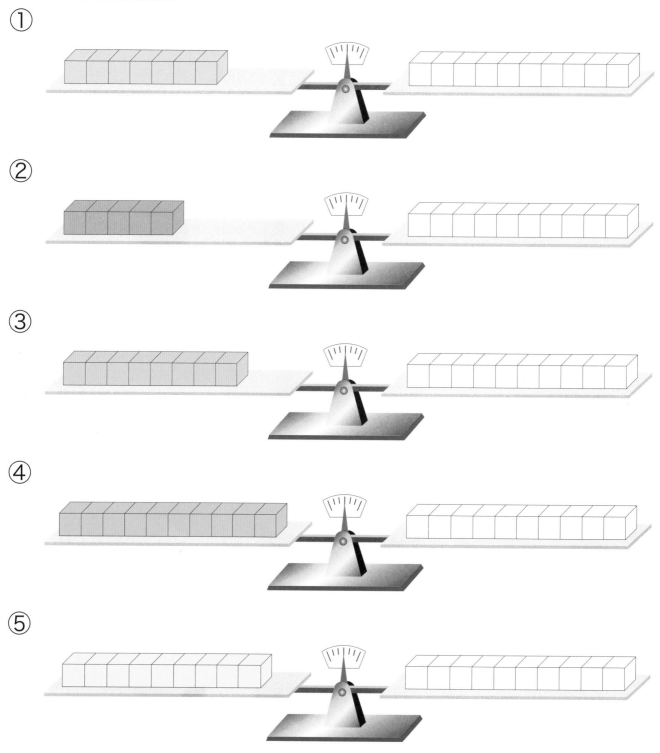

②

③

④

⑤

13 Equal Weights

■Each block below is the same size and weight. Color the correct number of blocks on the right side to match the weight of the blocks on the left side.

①

②

③

④

⑤

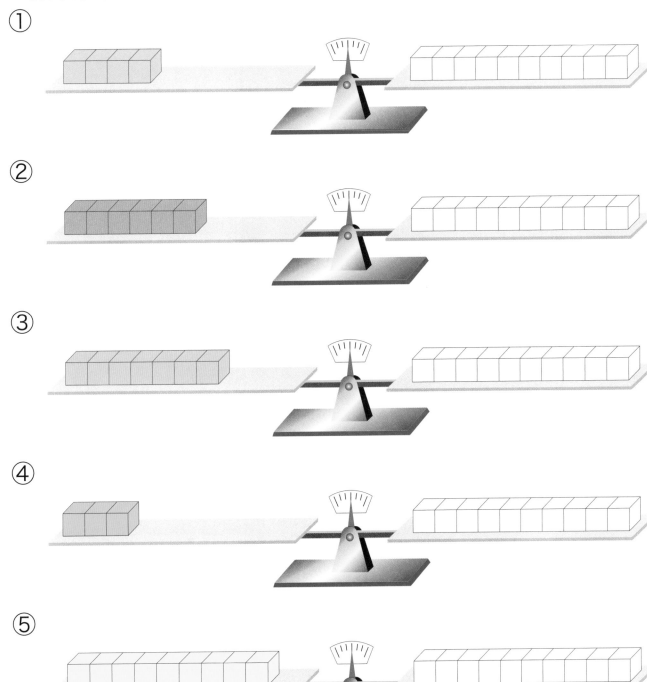

■Each block below is the same size and weight. Color the correct number of blocks on the right side to match the weight of the blocks on the left side.

①

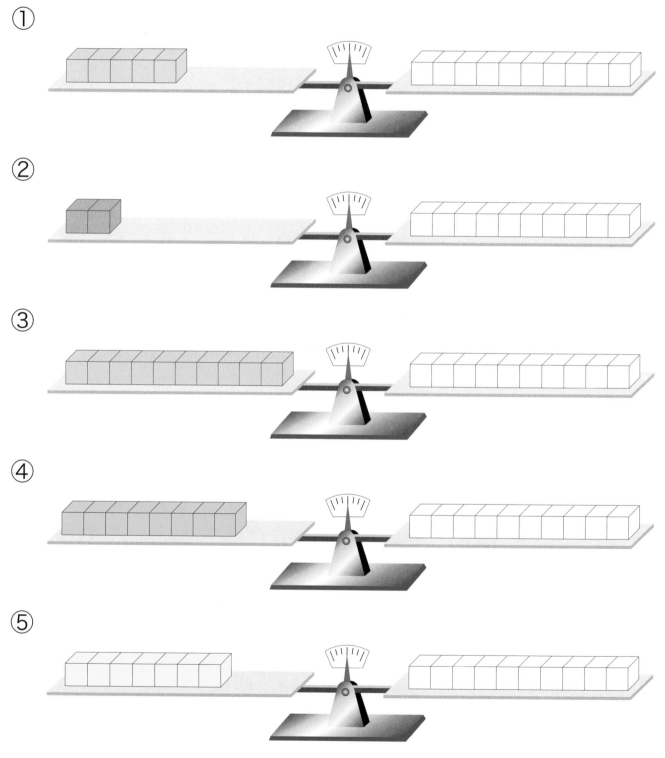

②

③

④

⑤

26

Review

14

Name	
Date	

■ Which object is heaviest? Circle the heaviest object.

①

②

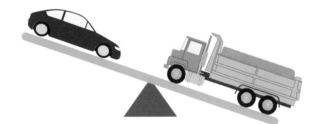   

③

   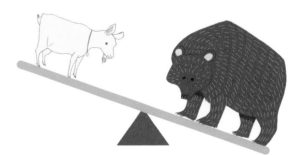

④

   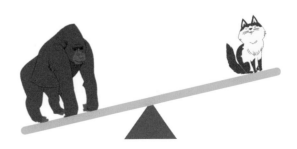

■Each block below is the same size and weight. Which is the heaviest group, and which is the lightest group below? Write a check (✔) under the heaviest and a circle (○) under the lightest.

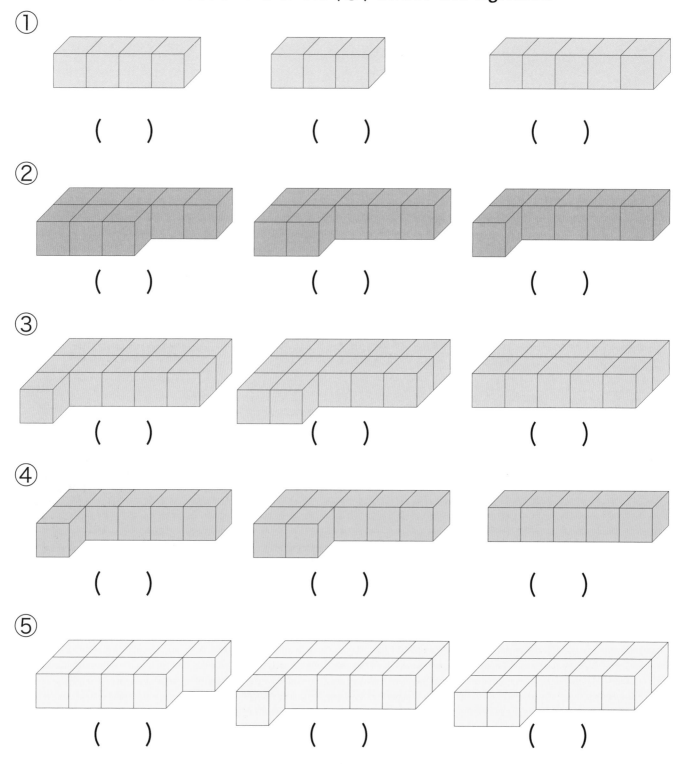

①   (   )   (   )   (   )

②   (   )   (   )   (   )

③   (   )   (   )   (   )

④   (   )   (   )   (   )

⑤   (   )   (   )   (   )

15 Practicing Numbers 1 to 100

Name

Date

■ Trace each number while saying it aloud.

1	2	3	4	5	6	7	8	9	10
11	12	13	14	15	16	17	18	19	20
21	22	23	24	25	26	27	28	29	30
31	32	33	34	35	36	37	38	39	40
41	42	43	44	45	46	47	48	49	50
51	52	53	54	55	56	57	58	59	60
61	62	63	64	65	66	67	68	69	70
71	72	73	74	75	76	77	78	79	80
81	82	83	84	85	86	87	88	89	90
91	92	93	94	95	96	97	98	99	100

■Trace each number while saying it aloud.

1	2	3	4	5	6	7	8	9	10
11	12	13	14	15	16	17	18	19	20
21	22	23	24	25	26	27	28	29	30
31	32	33	34	35	36	37	38	39	40
41	42	43	44	45	46	47	48	49	50
51	52	53	54	55	56	57	58	59	60
61	62	63	64	65	66	67	68	69	70
71	72	73	74	75	76	77	78	79	80
81	82	83	84	85	86	87	88	89	90
91	92	93	94	95	96	97	98	99	100

Practicing Numbers 1 to 100

Name

Date

■ Trace each number while saying it aloud.

1	2	3	4	5	6	7	8	9	10
11	12	13	14	15	16	17	18	19	20
21	22	23	24	25	26	27	28	29	30
31	32	33	34	35	36	37	38	39	40
41	42	43	44	45	46	47	48	49	50
51	52	53	54	55	56	57	58	59	60
61	62	63	64	65	66	67	68	69	70
71	72	73	74	75	76	77	78	79	80
81	82	83	84	85	86	87	88	89	90
91	92	93	94	95	96	97	98	99	100

■Write each number while saying it aloud.

1	2	3	4	5	6	7	8	9	10
11	12	13	14	15	16	17	18	19	20
21	22	23	24	25	26	27	28	29	30
31	32	33	34	35	36	37	38	39	40
41	42	43	44	45	46	47	48	49	50
51	52	53	54	55	56	57	58	59	60
61	62	63	64	65	66	67	68	69	70
71	72	73	74	75	76	77	78	79	80
81	82	83	84	85	86	87	88	89	90
91	92	93	94	95	96	97	98	99	100

17 Pounds

Name

Date

■ Read the weight on each scale and trace it below.

①

(1 lb.)

②

(2 lb.)

③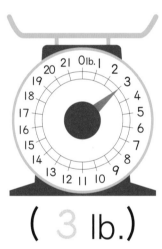

(3 lb.)

④

(4 lb.)

⑤

(5 lb.)

⑥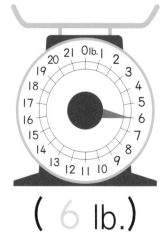

(6 lb.)

■Read the weight on each scale and write it below.

①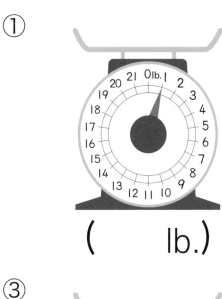

(lb.)

②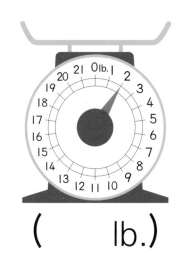

(lb.)

③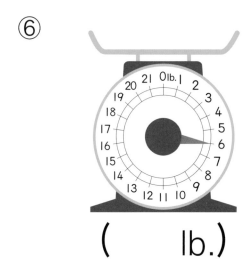

(lb.)

④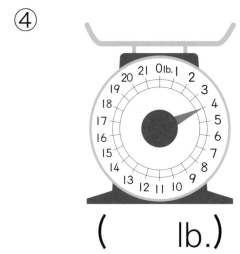

(lb.)

⑤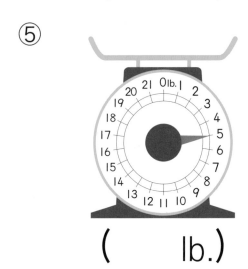

(lb.)

⑥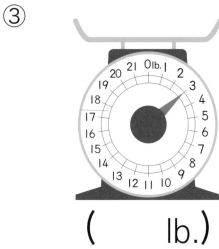

(lb.)

18 Pounds

Name

Date

■ Read the weight on each scale and trace it below.

①

(7 lb.)

②

(8 lb.)

③

(9 lb.)

④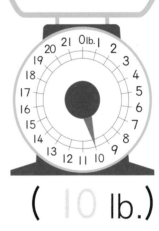

(10 lb.)

⑤

(11 lb.)

⑥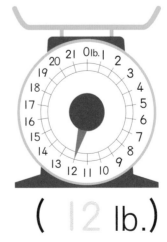

(12 lb.)

35

■Read the weight on each scale and write it below.

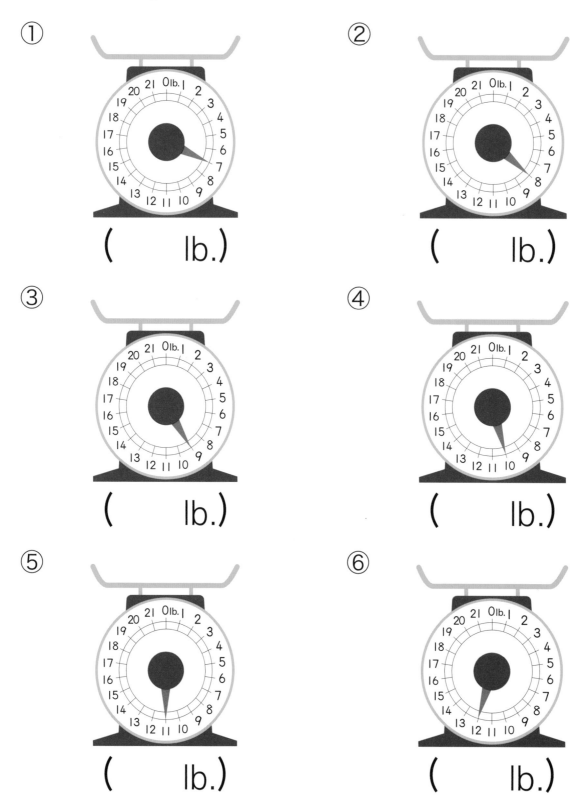

① (lb.)

② (lb.)

③ (lb.)

④ (lb.)

⑤ (lb.)

⑥ (lb.)

19 **Pounds**

Name

Date

■ Read the weight on each scale and trace it below.

①

(13 lb.)

②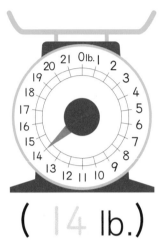

(14 lb.)

③

(15 lb.)

④

(16 lb.)

⑤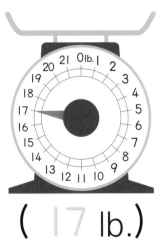

(17 lb.)

⑥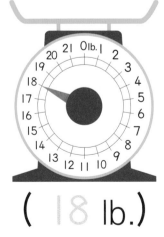

(18 lb.)

37

■Read the weight on each scale and write it below.

①

(lb.)

②

(lb.)

③

(lb.)

④

(lb.)

⑤

(lb.)

⑥

(lb.)

20 Pounds

Name

Date

■ Read the weight on each scale and trace it below.

①

(19 lb.)

②

(20 lb.)

③

(21 lb.)

④

(3 lb.)

⑤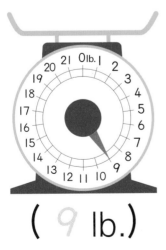

(9 lb.)

⑥

(15 lb.)

■Read the weight on each scale and write it below.

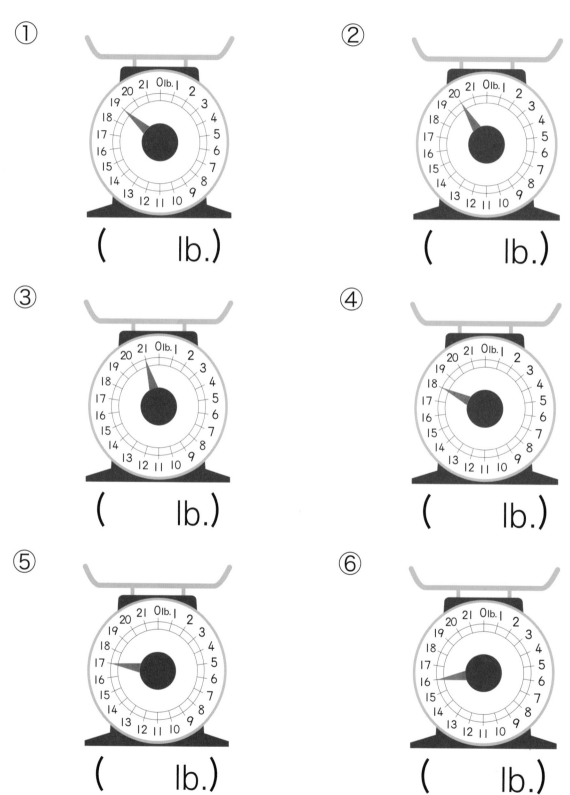

① (　　　lb.)

② (　　　lb.)

③ (　　　lb.)

④ (　　　lb.)

⑤ (　　　lb.)

⑥ (　　　lb.)

21 Pounds

■ Read the weight on each scale and write it below.

①

(lb.)

②

(lb.)

③

(lb.)

④

(lb.)

⑤

(lb.)

⑥

(lb.)

■Read the weight on each scale and write it below.

①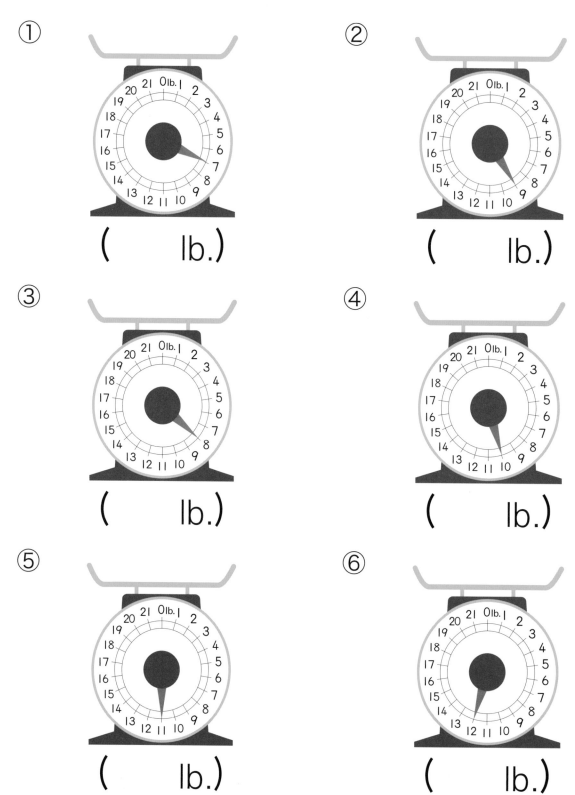

    (lb.)

②

    (lb.)

③

    (lb.)

④

    (lb.)

⑤

    (lb.)

⑥

    (lb.)

22 **Pounds**

Name

Date

■ Read the weight on each scale and write it below.

①

(　　　 lb.)

②

(　　　 lb.)

③

(　　　 lb.)

④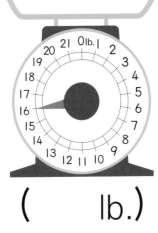

(　　　 lb.)

⑤

(　　　 lb.)

⑥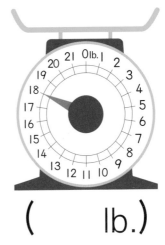

(　　　 lb.)

43

■Read the weight on each scale and write it below.

①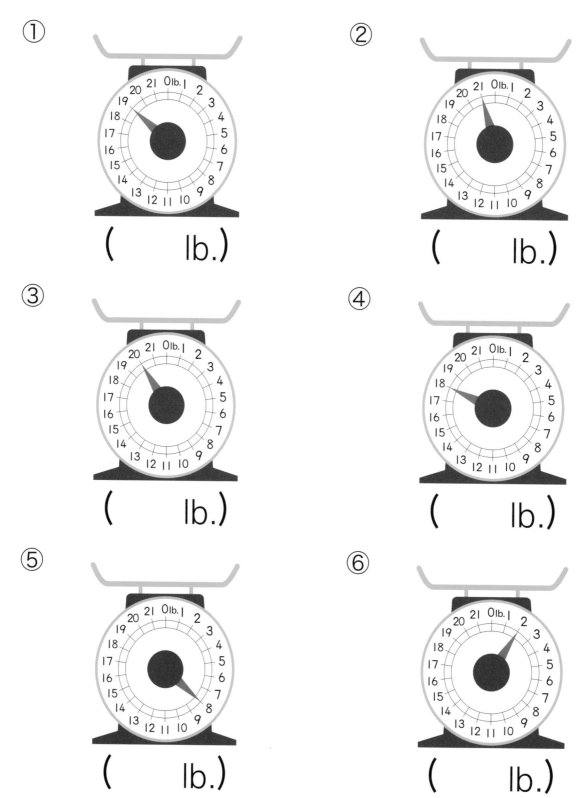

(lb.)

②

(lb.)

③

(lb.)

④

(lb.)

⑤

(lb.)

⑥

(lb.)

Name

Date

■ Read the weight on each scale and write it below.

①

(lb.)

②

(lb.)

③

(lb.)

④

(lb.)

⑤

(lb.)

⑥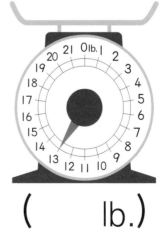

(lb.)

■Read the weight on each scale and write it below.

①

(lb.)

②

(lb.)

③

(lb.)

④

(lb.)

⑤

(lb.)

⑥

(lb.)

24 Pounds

■ Read the weight on each scale and write it below.

①

(lb.)

②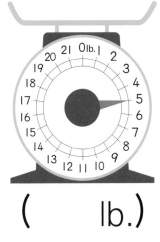

(lb.)

③

(lb.)

④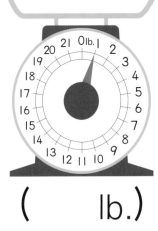

(lb.)

⑤

(lb.)

⑥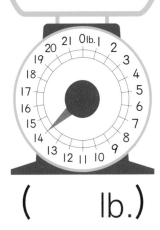

(lb.)

■Read the weight on each scale and write it below.

①

(lb.)

②

(lb.)

③

(lb.)

④

(lb.)

⑤

(lb.)

⑥

(lb.)

 **Pounds**

Name

Date

■Read the weight on each scale and write it below.

①

(lb.)

②

(lb.)

③

(lb.)

④

(lb.)

⑤

(lb.)

⑥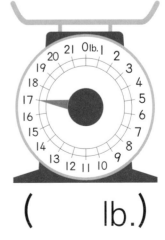

(lb.)

■Read the weight on each scale and write it below.

①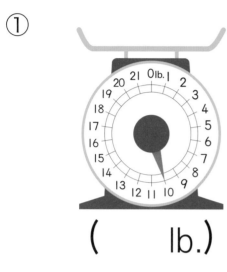

(　　　 lb.)

②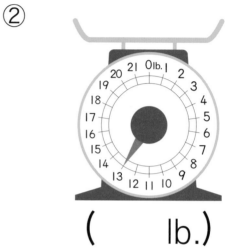

(　　　 lb.)

③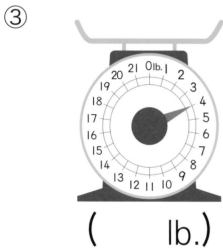

(　　　 lb.)

④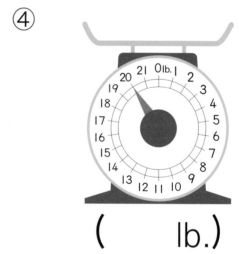

(　　　 lb.)

⑤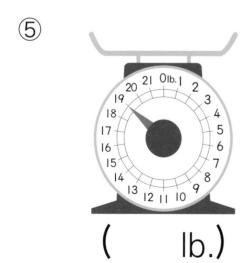

(　　　 lb.)

⑥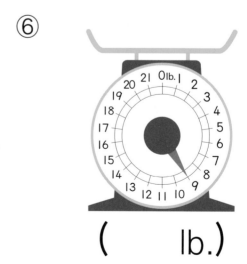

(　　　 lb.)

Review
Pounds

Name

Date

■ Read the weight on each scale and write it below.

①

(lb.)

②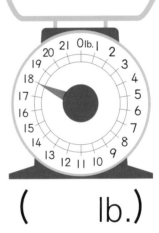

(lb.)

③

(lb.)

④

(lb.)

⑤

(lb.)

⑥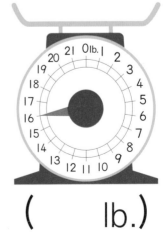

(lb.)

■Read the weight on each scale and write it below.

①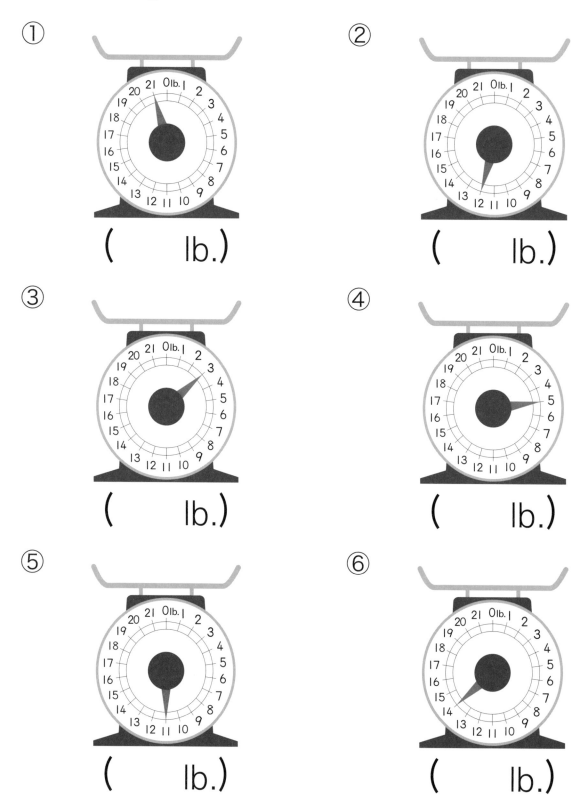

(　　　 lb.)

②

(　　　 lb.)

③

(　　　 lb.)

④

(　　　 lb.)

⑤

(　　　 lb.)

⑥

(　　　 lb.)

■ Trace each number while saying it aloud.

51	52	53	54	55	56	57	58	59	60
61	62	63	64	65	66	67	68	69	70
71	72	73	74	75	76	77	78	79	80
81	82	83	84	85	86	87	88	89	90
91	92	93	94	95	96	97	98	99	100
101	102	103	104	105	106	107	108	109	110
111	112	113	114	115	116	117	118	119	120
121	122	123	124	125	126	127	128	129	130
131	132	133	134	135	136	137	138	139	140
141	142	143	144	145	146	147	148	149	150

■ Trace each number while saying it aloud.

101	102	103	104	105	106	107	108	109	110
111	112	113	114	115	116	117	118	119	120
121	122	123	124	125	126	127	128	129	130
131	132	133	134	135	136	137	138	139	140
141	142	143	144	145	146	147	148	149	150
151	152	153	154	155	156	157	158	159	160
161	162	163	164	165	166	167	168	169	170
171	172	173	174	175	176	177	178	179	180
181	182	183	184	185	186	187	188	189	190
191	192	193	194	195	196	197	198	199	200

28 Grams

■ Read the weight on each scale and trace it below.

①

(10 g)

②

(20 g)

③

(30 g)

④

(40 g)

⑤

(50 g)

⑥

(60 g)

■Read the weight on each scale and write it below.

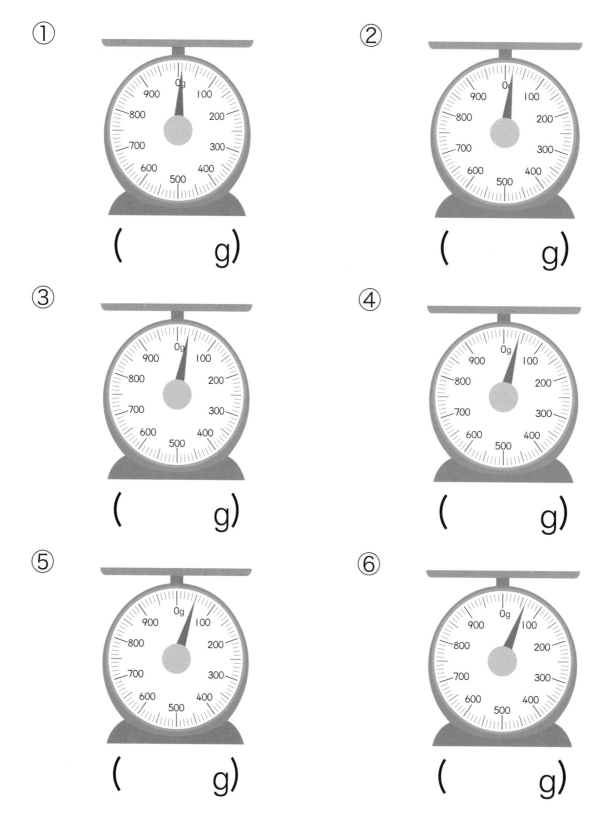

① (g)

② (g)

③ (g)

④ (g)

⑤ (g)

⑥ (g)

29 Grams

Name

Date

■Read the weight on each scale and trace it below.

①

(70 g)

②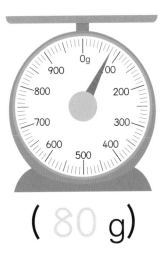

(80 g)

③

(90 g)

④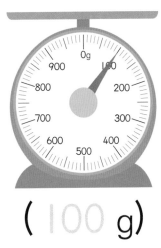

(100 g)

⑤

(110 g)

⑥

(120 g)

Read the weight on each scale and write it below.

①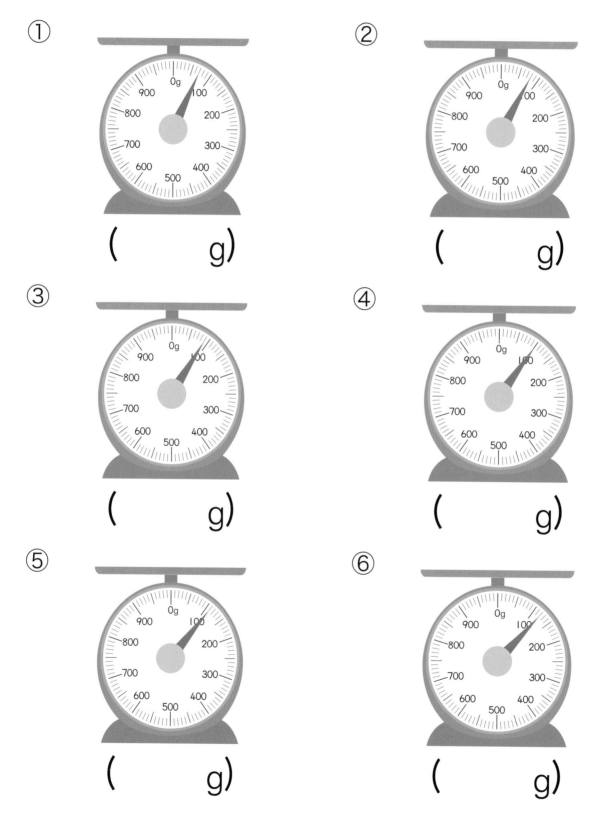

(g)

②

(g)

③

(g)

④

(g)

⑤

(g)

⑥

(g)

30 Grams

Name

Date

■ Read the weight on each scale and trace it below.

①

(130 g)

②

(140 g)

③

(150 g)

④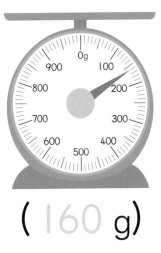

(160 g)

⑤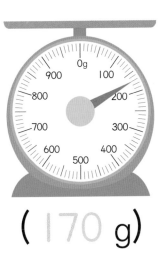

(170 g)

⑥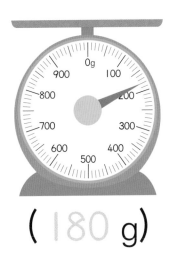

(180 g)

Read the weight on each scale and write it below.

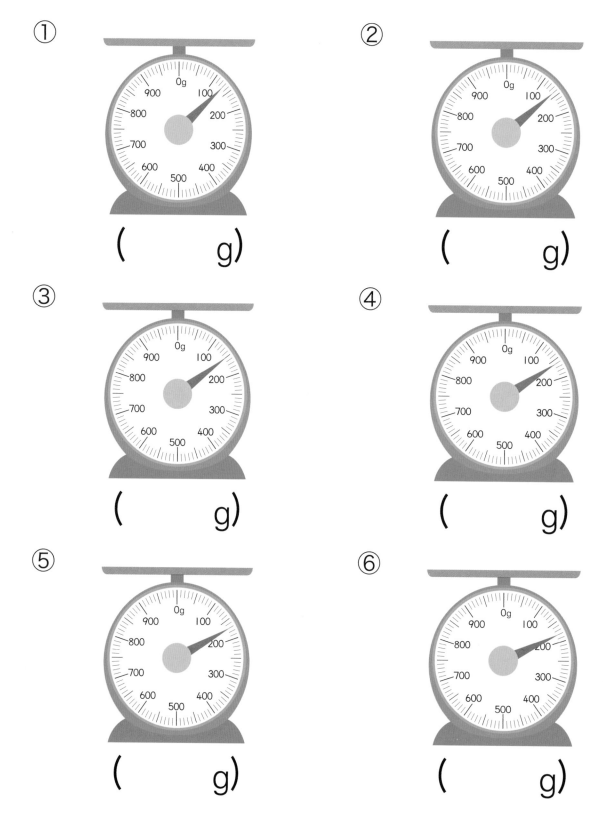

① (g)

② (g)

③ (g)

④ (g)

⑤ (g)

⑥ (g)

31 Grams

■ Read the weight on each scale and trace it below.

①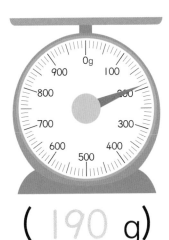

(190 g)

②

(200 g)

③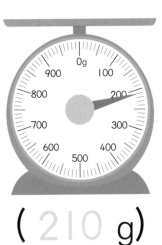

(210 g)

④

(220 g)

⑤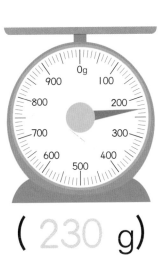

(230 g)

⑥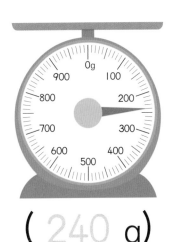

(240 g)

■Read the weight on each scale and write it below.

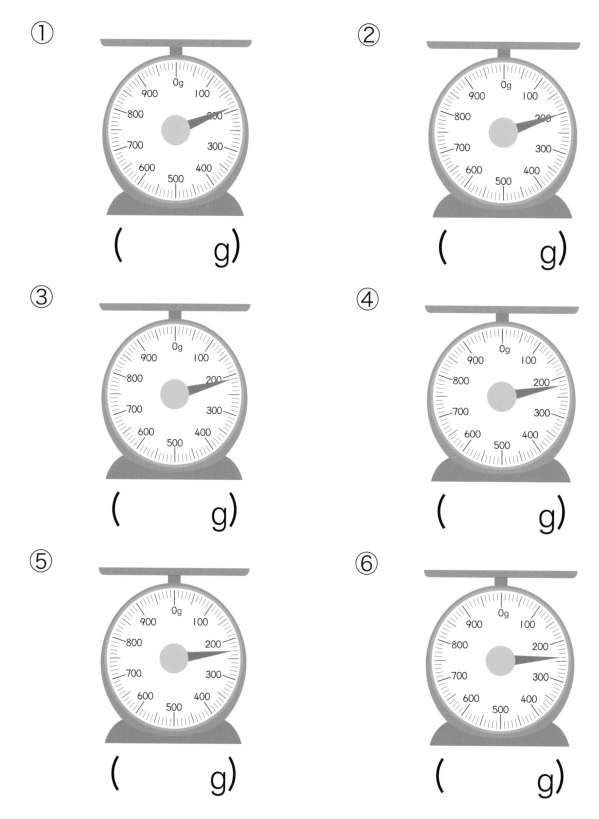

① (g)

② (g)

③ (g)

④ (g)

⑤ (g)

⑥ (g)

32 Grams

■Read the weight on each scale and trace it below.

①

(250 g)

②

(260 g)

③

(270 g)

④

(280 g)

⑤

(290 g)

⑥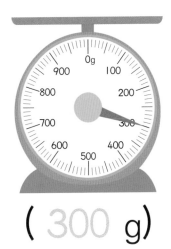

(300 g)

■Read the weight on each scale and write it below.

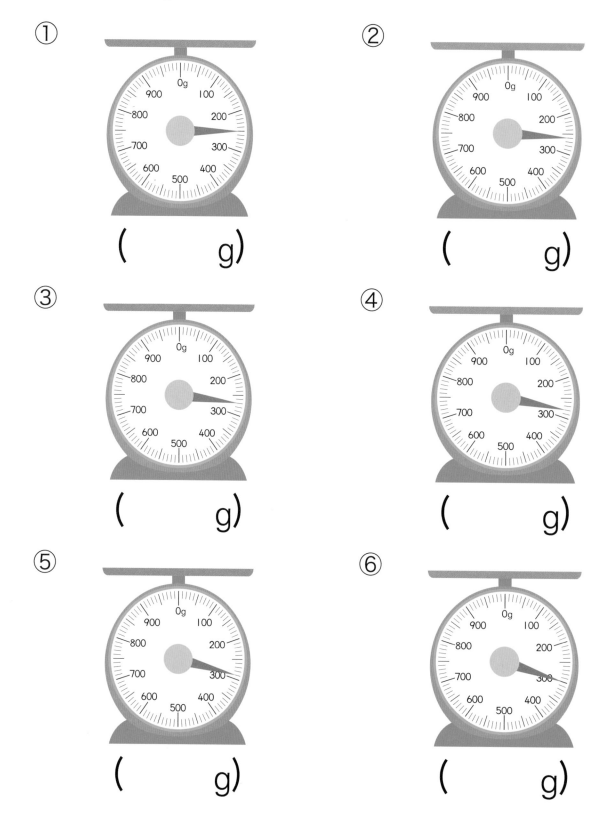

① (g)

② (g)

③ (g)

④ (g)

⑤ (g)

⑥ (g)

33 Grams

Name

Date

■ Read the weight on each scale and trace it below.

①

(100 g)

②

(200 g)

③

(300 g)

④

(400 g)

⑤

(500 g)

⑥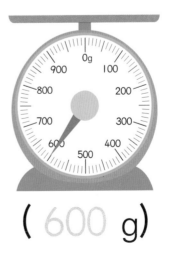

(600 g)

■Read the weight on each scale and write it below.

①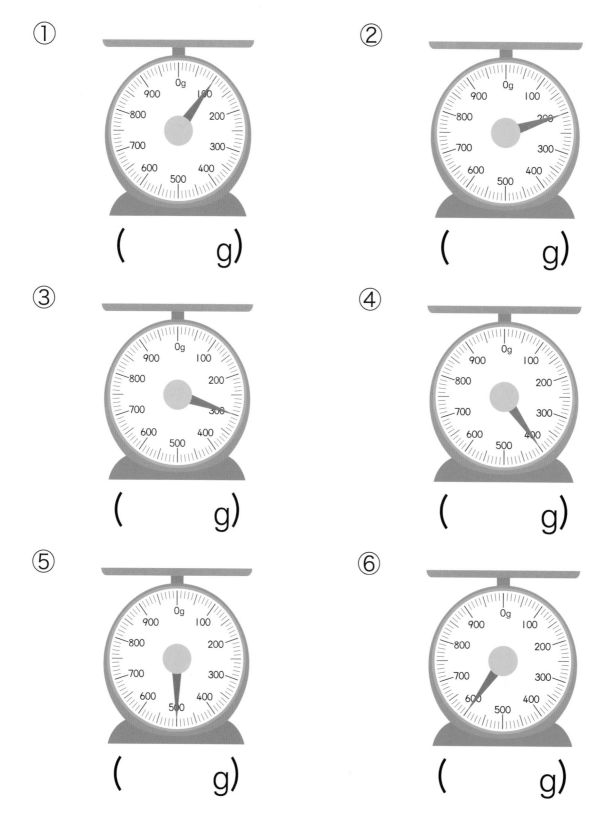

(g)

②

(g)

③

(g)

④

(g)

⑤

(g)

⑥

(g)

34 Grams

Name

Date

■ Read the weight on each scale and trace it below.

①

(700 g)

②

(800 g)

③

(900 g)

④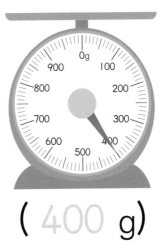

(400 g)

⑤

(600 g)

⑥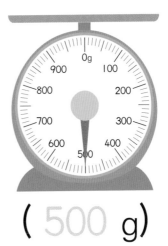

(500 g)

■Read the weight on each scale and write it below.

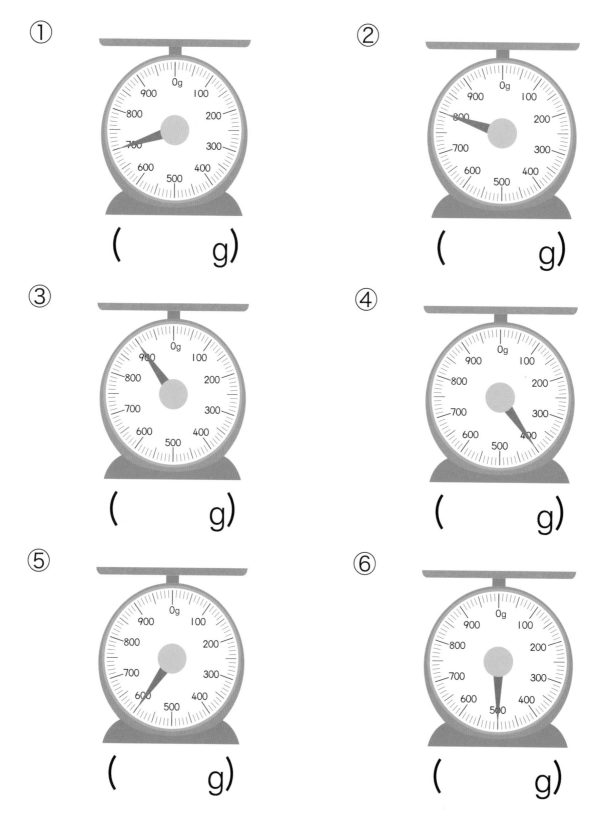

① (g)

② (g)

③ (g)

④ (g)

⑤ (g)

⑥ (g)

35 Grams

Name

Date

■ Read the weight on each scale and write it below.

①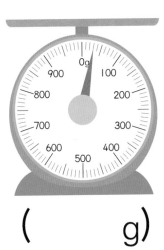

(g)

②

(g)

③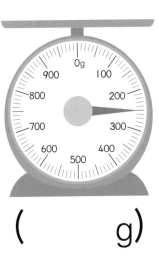

(g)

④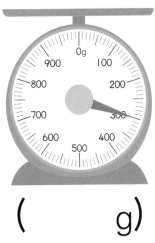

(g)

⑤

(g)

⑥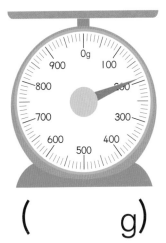

(g)

■Read the weight on each scale and write it below.

①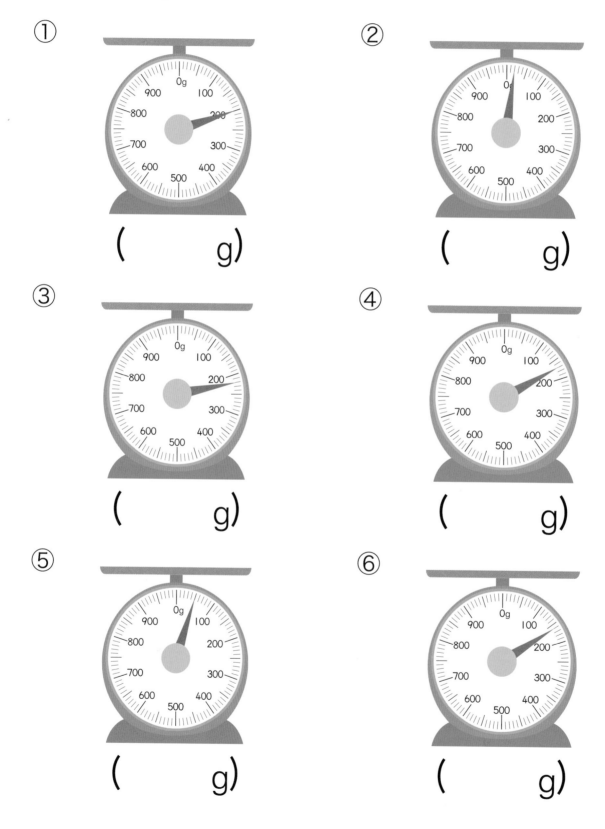

(g)

② (g)

③ (g)

④ (g)

⑤ (g)

⑥ (g)

36 Grams

Name

Date

■ Read the weight on each scale and write it below.

①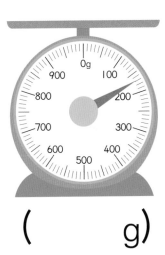

(g)

②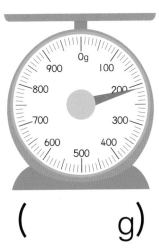

(g)

③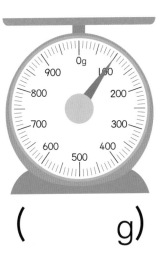

(g)

④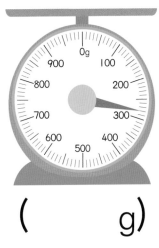

(g)

⑤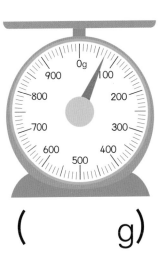

(g)

⑥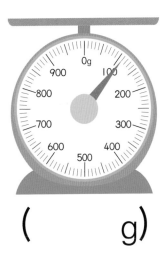

(g)

■Read the weight on each scale and write it below.

①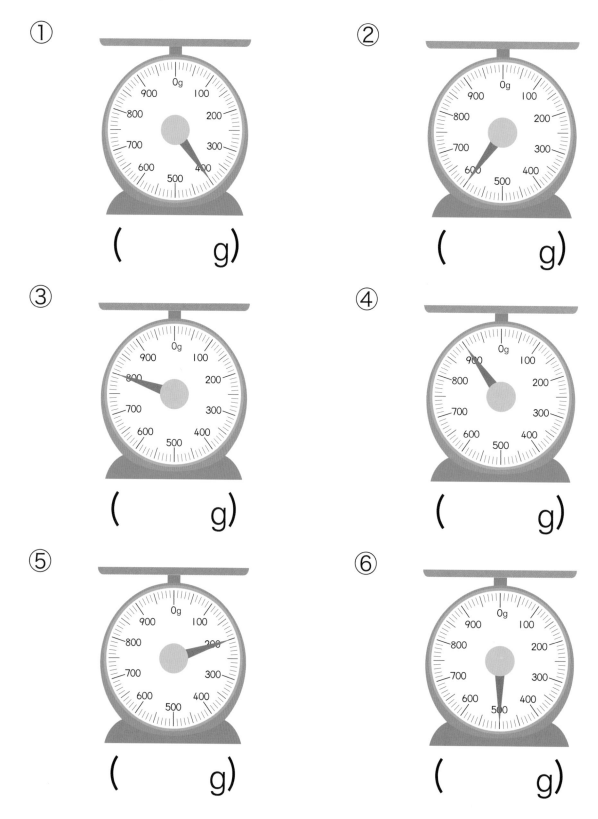

(g)

② (g)

③ (g)

④ (g)

⑤ (g)

⑥ (g)

Name

Date

■Read the weight on each scale and write it below.

①

(g)

②

(g)

③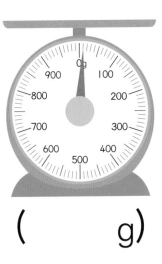

(g)

④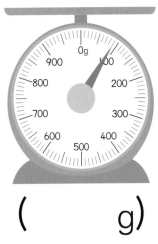

(g)

⑤

(g)

⑥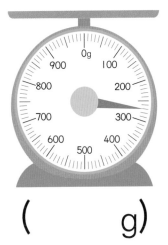

(g)

■Read the weight on each scale and write it below.

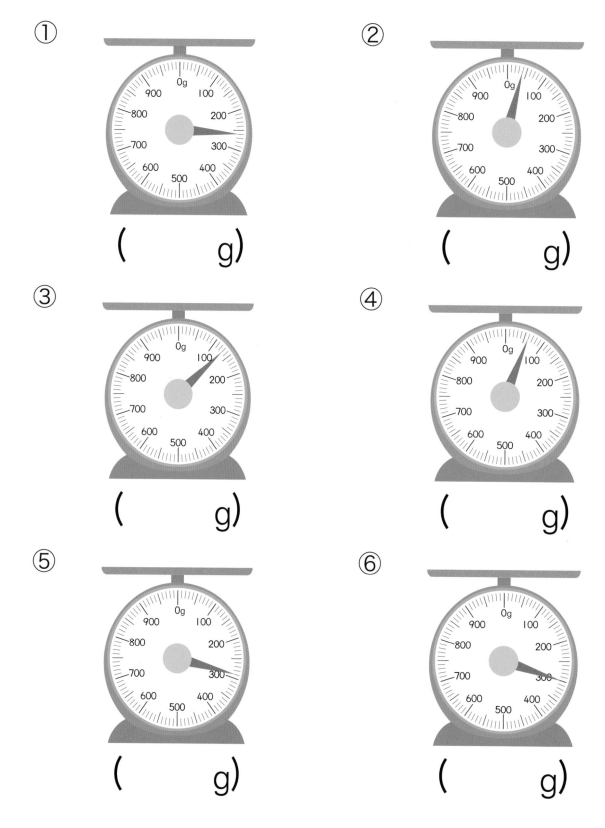

① (g)

② (g)

③ (g)

④ (g)

⑤ (g)

⑥ (g)

Name

Date

■Read the weight on each scale and write it below.

①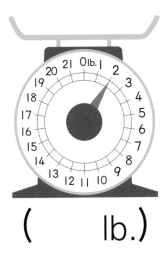

(lb.)

②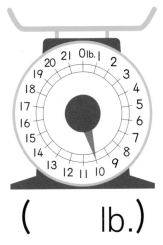

(lb.)

③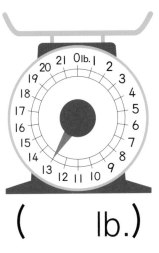

(lb.)

④

(lb.)

⑤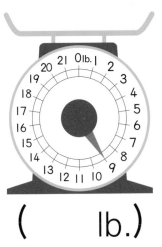

(lb.)

⑥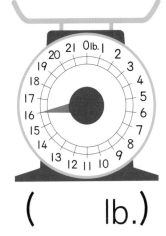

(lb.)

■Read the weight on each scale and write it below.

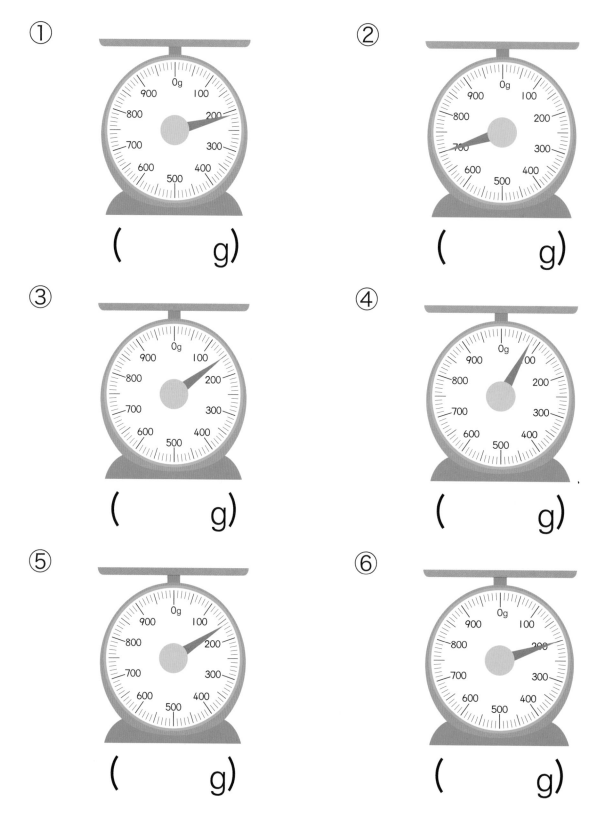

① (　　　　　g)

② (　　　　　g)

③ (　　　　　g)

④ (　　　　　g)

⑤ (　　　　　g)

⑥ (　　　　　g)

Certificate of Achievement

is hereby congratulated on completing

My Book of Measurement: Weight

Presented on _____, 20 _____

_____
Parent or Guardian